PIANO/VOCAL/GUITAR

SELECTIONS FROM

THE BEATLES

ANTHOLOGY

3

ISBN 0-7935-7536-2

HAL•LEONARD®
CORPORATION
7777 W. BLUEMOUND RD. P.O. BOX 13819 MILWAUKEE, WI 53213

Visit Hal Leonard Online at
www.halleonard.com

GLASS ONION

Words and Music by JOHN LENNON
and PAUL McCARTNEY

Moderate rock beat

2 The Verse 1 lyrics are used for all three verses.

3 "Anthology 3" lyrics: "Well, here's a place you know just as real."

4 "Anthology 3" lyrics: "It's just another place you can go, wo."

The version of the song released on "Anthology 3" differs from the standard version, printed here, as annotated.

1 The "Anthology 3" version begins with 2 measures of C major and then continues with p.8, system 1, m.1 ("I told you 'bout").

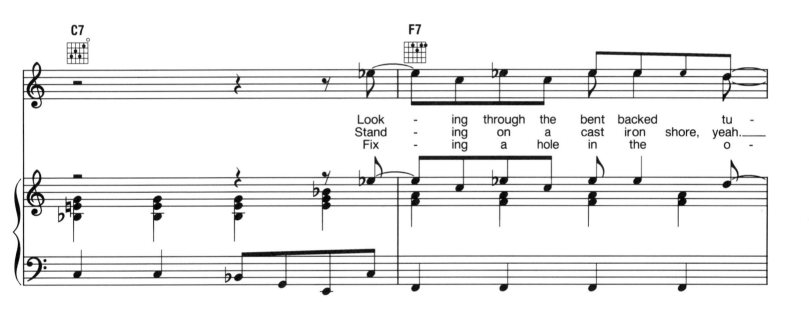

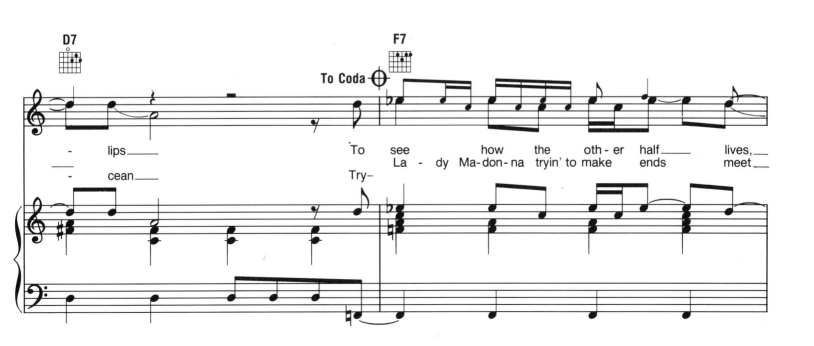

Look - ing through a glass o - nion.___
yeah,___ Look - ing through a glass o - nion.___

oh   yeah___

Oh

yeah   Oh

5 During Verse 2, two measures of A minor are added after this measure, then to p.8, system 1, m.1 ("I told you 'bout").

6 During Verse 3, the "Anthology 3" version fades out with spoken words and syllables after this measure.

JUNK

Words and Music by
PAUL McCARTNEY

The version of the song released on "Anthology 3" differs from the standard version, printed here, as annotated.

1 The "Anthology 3" version is in F minor.

2 After this measure, to p.12, 1st system, m.1. The Verse 1 lyrics are then repeated.

3 After this measure, to p.13, 3rd system, m.3 ("Buy, buy").

4 After this measure, to p.13, 1st system, m.1. The vocals are omitted through the last measure of the "Anthology 3" version (p.13, 3rd system, m.1).

PIGGIES

Words and Music by
GEORGE HARRISON

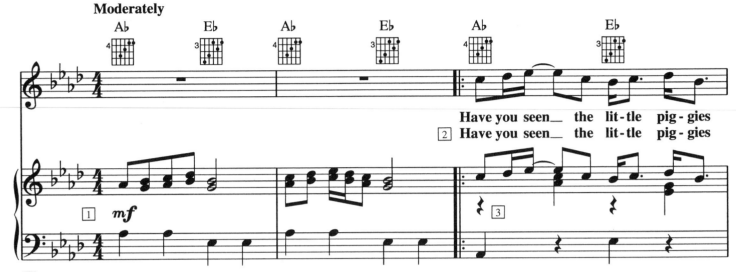

Moderately

Have you seen__ the lit-tle pig-gies
2 Have you seen__ the lit-tle pig-gies

1 mf

1 The "Anthology 3" version is in G major.

2 "Anthology 3" Verse 2 lyrics: "Have you seen the bigger piggies."

3 The "Anthology 3" version begins at this measure.

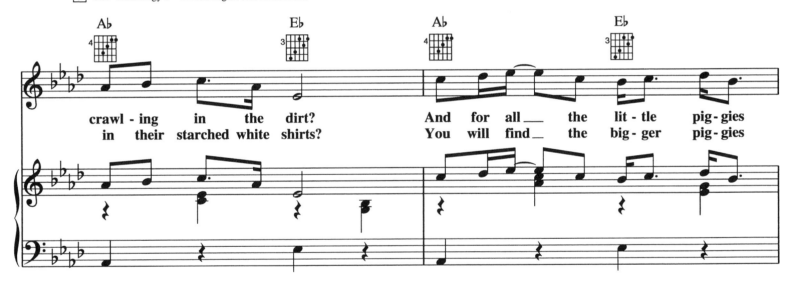

crawl-ing in the dirt? And for all__ the lit-tle pig-gies
in their starched white shirts? You will find__ the big-ger pig-gies

life is get-ting worse, al-ways hav-ing dirt to
stir-ring up the dirt, al-ways have clean shirts to

The version of the song released on "Anthology 3" differs from the standard version, printed here, as annotated.

18

4 The melody from p.16 is whistled until the lyrics return on p.19.

5 "Anthology 3" lyrics: "Pick up their pork chops."

6 The first chord in this measure and the next measure is G major.

7 The "Anthology 3" version ends with this measure. The chord progression is G (beat 1), D (beat 2), and G (beat 3). The lyrics are omitted.

OB-LA-DI, OB-LA-DA

Words and Music by JOHN LENNON
and PAUL McCARTNEY

[1] The "Anthology 3" version is in A major.

[2] The "Anthology 3" version begins at this measure.

The version of the song released on "Anthology 3" differs from the standard version, printed here, as annotated.

3 The Verse 2 lyrics are the same as the Verse 1 lyrics.

5 The vocals are omitted in this measure only, then to p.25, 4th system, m.2 ("Ob-la-di-bla-da").

GOOD NIGHT
(SUPPLEMENT)

To p.27, 3rd system, m.1

[1] This is a transcription of the beginning of the "Anthology 3" version. This version then continues with p.27, 3rd system, m.1.

GOOD NIGHT

Words and Music by JOHN LENNON
and PAUL McCARTNEY

Slowly and dreamily

The version of the song released on "Anthology 3" differs from the standard version, printed here, as annotated.

[1] See supplement for the beginning of the "Anthology 3" version.   [2] The Cmaj7 chord is replaced with Am7 in the "Anthology 3" version.

3 The Cmaj7 chord is replaced with Am7 in the "Anthology 3" version.

CRY BABY CRY

Words and Music by JOHN LENNON
and PAUL McCARTNEY

1 The "Anthology 3" version begins with 2 measures of G major and then continues with this measure.

2 The "Anthology 3" version omits the vocals "She's old enough to know better."

The version of the song released on "Anthology 3" differs from the standard version, printed here, as annotated.

BLACKBIRD

Words and Music by JOHN LENNON
and PAUL McCARTNEY

34

Black - bird,— fly,—

[1] This measure is repeated, then to p.36, 1st system, m.2 ("Blackbird singing in the dead of night").

Black - bird,— fly,— in - to the

light of a dark, black night.—

[2] After this measure, to p.36, 2nd system, m.1 ("Take these broken wings"). The vocals are omitted in m.1-2, but re-enter in m.3. The "Anthology 3" version then continues, as written, and fades out after p.36, 4th system, m.1.

molto rit.   a tempo

The version of the song released on "Anthology 3" differs from the standard version, printed here, as annotated.

⌐3⌐ After this measure, to p.35, 1st system, m.4 ("Blackbird, fly").

WHILE MY GUITAR GENTLY WEEPS

Words and Music by
GEORGE HARRISON

[1] This is a transcription of the "Anthology 3" version of the song.

HEY JUDE

Words and Music by JOHN LENNON
and PAUL McCARTNEY

The version of the song released on "Anthology 3" differs from the standard version, printed here, as annotated.

1 "Anthology 3" D.S. lyrics: "Into your heart, then you can start."

42

"Anthology 3" Verse 2 lyrics: "She has found you, go out and get her."

NOT GUILTY

Words and Music by
GEORGE HARRISON

The version of the song released on "Anthology 3" differs from the standard version, printed here, as annotated.

[1] The chord progression of Em7, Em6, Cmaj7/E is replaced with a single Em chord throughout the "Anthology 3" version.

[2] After this measure, an extra measure of 4/4, containing an E7 chord in the accompaniment and a tied whole-note B in the vocals, has been added.

3 After this measure, to p.46, 1st system, m.1. The "Anthology 3" version then continues with the lyrics from Verse 2.

4 This measure is omitted, and the vocals are moved to the next measure.

5 The vocals are omitted until the 2nd ending. Also, a guitar solo begins in the next measure.

6 This measure is repeated during the second time through this section.

7 The vocals are omitted in this measure. The "Anthology 3" version then returns to p.47, 4th system, m.1.

8 M.2-3 in this system are repeated several times. The vocals are also omitted. The "Anthology 3" version ends by fading out during the repeated measures.

MOTHER NATURE'S SON

Words and Music by JOHN LENNON
and PAUL McCARTNEY

The version of the song released on "Anthology 3" differs from the standard version, printed here, as annotated.

1 The "Anthology 3" version begins here and omits the next measure. 2 During the D.S. verse, the instrumental solo is omitted. Instead, "Du" is sung with each melody note.

3 After this measure in the D.S. verse, to p.51, 1st system, m.1 ("Du du").

4 This measure and the next measure are omitted from the "Anthology 3" version.

Du du du du du du du du du du du

du du du du du du du du du,

du du du.

1 D

5

D

D.S. al Coda

CODA

(Hum) Moth-er Na-ture's son.

5 The "Anthology 3" version ends with this measure.

I'M SO TIRED

Words and Music by JOHN LENNON
and PAUL McCARTNEY

I'm so tired, I have-n't slept a wink, I'm
so tired, I don't know what to do, I'm

so tired, my mind is on the blink.
so tired, my mind is set on you.

I

won-der should I get up and fix my-self a drink, no, no, no. I'm

I WILL

Words and Music by JOHN LENNON
and PAUL McCARTNEY

56

The version of the song released on "Anthology 3" differs from the standard version, printed here, as annotated.

1 The vocal harmony is omitted in the "Anthology 3" version.

2 "Anthology 3" lyrics: "Love you with all my heart."

3 "Anthology 3" lyrics: "For the things you do endear me to you."

WHY DON'T WE DO IT IN THE ROAD

Words and Music by JOHN LENNON
and PAUL McCARTNEY

Moderately

Why don't we do it in the road?_____

1 This section is repeated five times, and the first ending is taken each time.

2 At the beginning of Verse 5, the first two beats of this measure are played,
and then the "Anthology 3" version ends.

Why don't we do it in the road?_____

Why don't we do it in the road?_____   Why don't we do it in the road?__

The version of the song released on "Anthology 3" differs from the standard version, printed here, as annotated.

I'VE GOT A FEELING

Words and Music by JOHN LENNON
and PAUL McCARTNEY

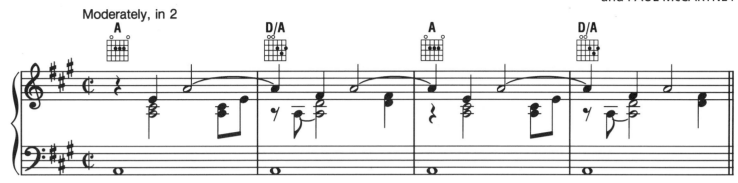

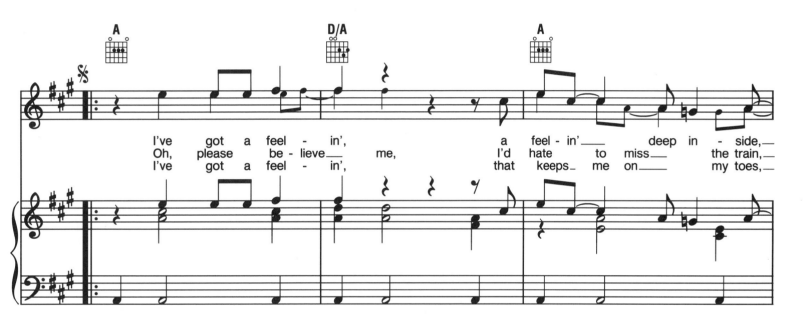

I've got a feel-in', a feel-in'____ deep in-side,____
Oh, please be-lieve____ me, I'd hate to miss____ the train,____
I've got a feel-in', that keeps____ me on____ my toes,____

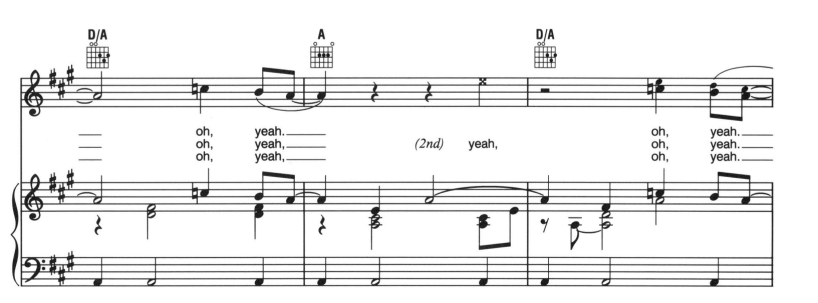

____ oh, yeah.____
____ oh, yeah,____ (2nd) yeah, oh, yeah.____
oh, yeah,____ oh, yeah.____

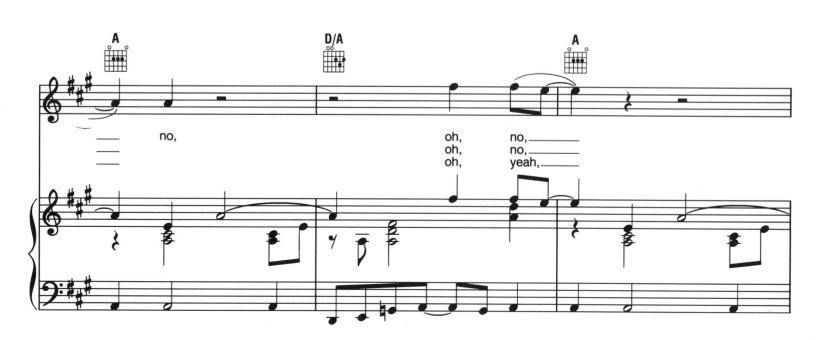

The version of the song released on "Anthology 3" differs from the standard version, printed here, as annotated.

1 "Anthology 3" Verse 2 lyrics: "Everybody had a hard year, everybody got their feet up, everybody let their hair down, everybody put their socks up."

TWO OF US

Words and Music by JOHN LENNON
and PAUL McCARTNEY

1 The next four measures are repeated before Verse 1, but not before the other verses.

1. Two of us, rid - ing no - where, spend - ing some -
2. Two of us, send - ing post - cards, writ - ing some let -
3,4. Two of us, wear - ing rain - coats, stand - ing so -

- one's hard - earned pay.
- ers, on my wall.
- lo, in the sun.

The version of the song released on "Anthology 3" differs from the standard version, printed here, as annotated.

You and me, Sun - day driv - ing,
You and me, burn - ing match - es,
You and me, chas - ing pa - per,

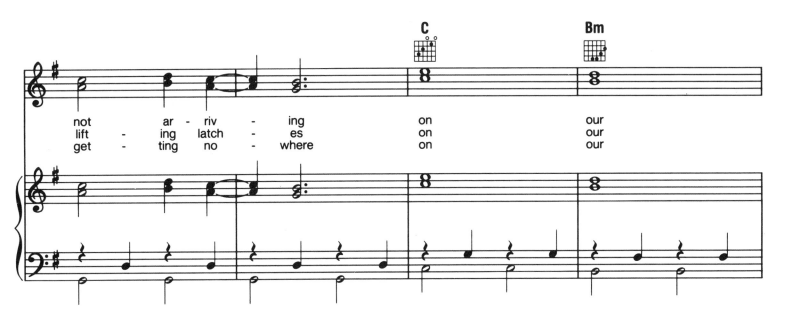

not - ar - riv - ing on our
lift - ing latch - es on our
get - ting no - where on our

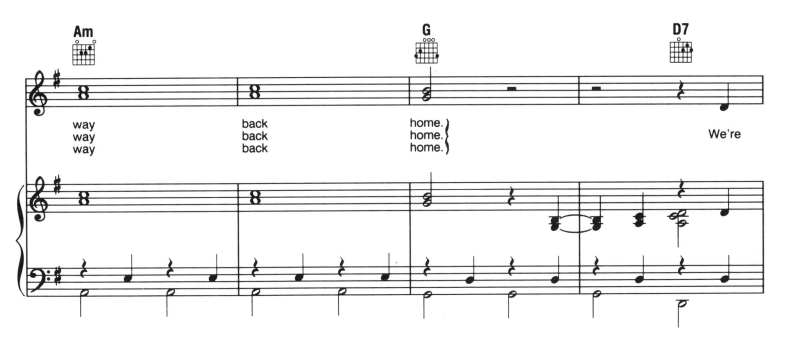

way back home.
way back home.
way back home.

We're

2 This chord is C major in the "Anthology 3" version.

the road___ that stretch - es out___ a - head.___

(Spoken:) We're go-in' home.   Better believe it.   Goodbye.

FOR YOU BLUE

Words and Music by
GEORGE HARRISON

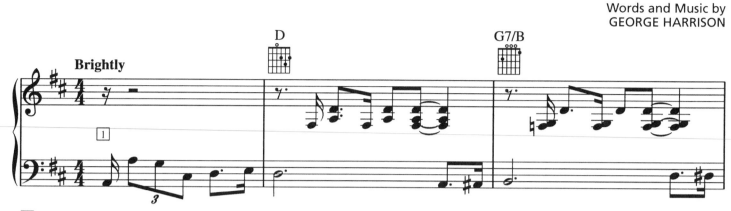

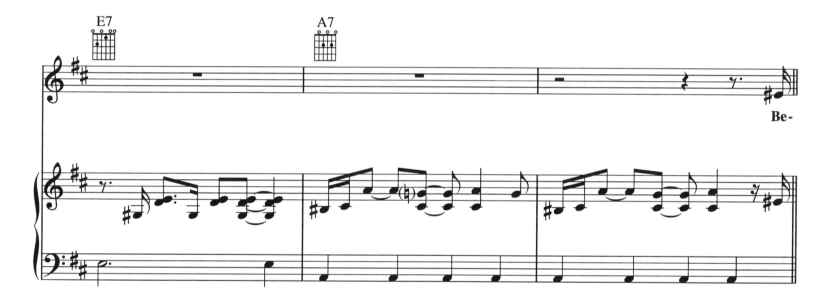

1 The "Anthology 3" version begins with the 11 measure chord progression D7 G7 D7 D7 G7 G7 D7 D7 A7 G7 D7. The song
   then continues at p.72, system 2, m.3.

2 "Anthology 3" Verse 3 lyrics: "Moment that I saw you."

(1.,4.) cause you're sweet __ and love - ly, girl,   I love you. __
(2.) want   you in ___ the morn - ing, girl,   I love you. __
(3.) loved you from __ the mo - ment __   I saw you. __ 2

The version of the song released on "Anthology 3" differs from the standard version, printed here, as annotated.

3 "Anthology 3" Verse 1 lyrics: "Because you're sweet and lovely, girl, I do."

4 "Anthology 3" Verse 4 lyrics: "I love you more each moment I'm with you."

5 "Anthology 3" Verse 1 lyrics: "Ever, girl, it's true."

(Spoken:) *Elmore James got nothin' on this baby.*

D.S. al Coda

Give it the blues.

CODA

8 The vocals are omitted, and all of the chords are changed to D7 in this measure and the next measure.

THE LONG AND WINDING ROAD

Words and Music by JOHN LENNON
and PAUL McCARTNEY

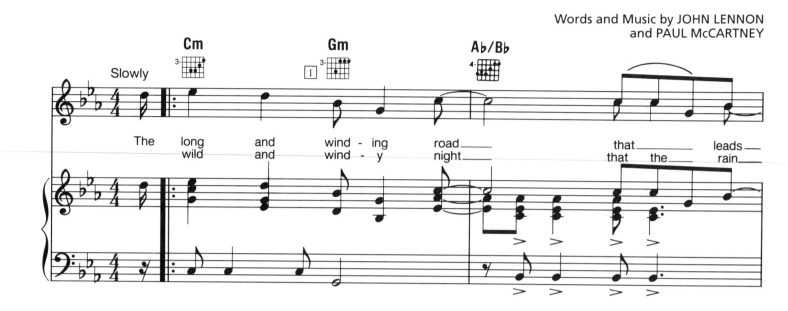

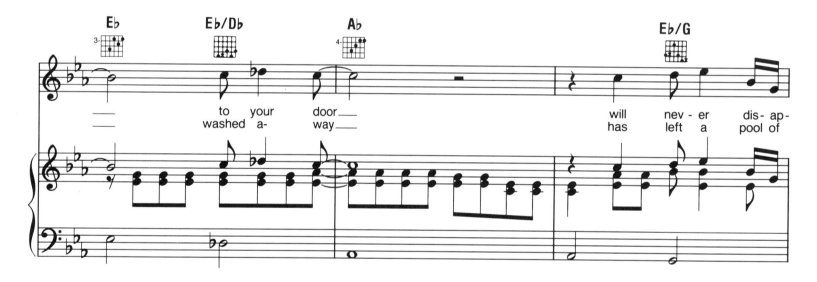

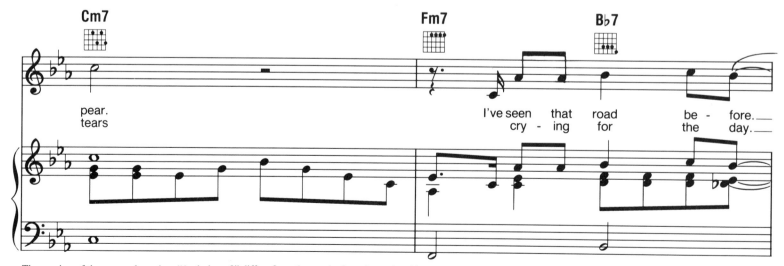

The version of the song released on "Anthology 3" differs from the standard version, printed here, as annotated.

[1] The G minor chord is omitted in the "Anthology 3" version.

3 After this measure, to p.77, system 3, m.2 ("Many times I've been alone"). The "Anthology 3" version then continues through p.78 and takes the Coda on p.79.

OH! DARLING

Words and Music by JOHN LENNON
and PAUL McCARTNEY

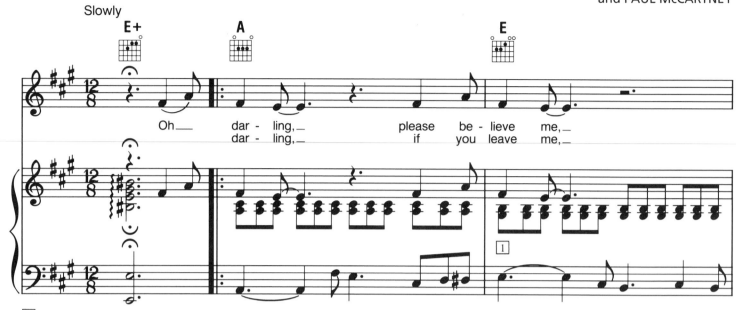

1 The "Anthology 3" version begins at this measure.

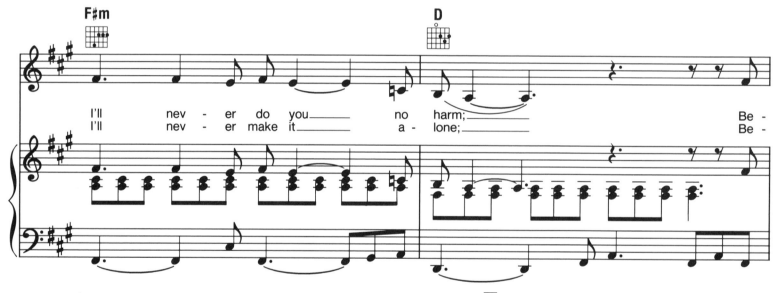

2 After Verse 1, the "Anthology 3" version takes the 2nd ending.

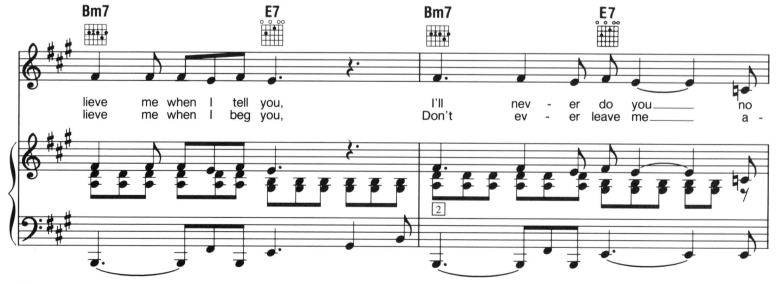

The version of the song released on "Anthology 3" differs from the standard version, printed here, as annotated.

3 "Anthology 3" lyrics: "Harm."

4 This chord is Dm7 in the "Anthology 3" version.

5 During the first time through this section, the "Anthology 3" lyrics are "Broke down and died."

6 "Anthology 3" lyrics: "I nearly broke down and died."

7 "Anthology 3" lyrics for all three verses: "Please believe me, I'll never do you no harm."

[8] To p.82, 3rd system, m.1 ("Darling, please believe me"). The "Anthology 3" version then continues, takes the 2nd ending, and ends with p.83, 3rd system, m.3.

ALL THINGS MUST PASS

Words and Music by
GEORGE HARRISON

The version of the song released on "Anthology 3" differs from the standard version, printed here, as annotated.

1 This measure's time signature is 3/4, and the vocals begin on beat 1.

2 The chord progression in the first ending is E, Esus(add9), E, A.

3 After this measure, there is an additional measure with an E major chord on beats 1-2 and an A major chord on beats 3-4.

4 The vocals are omitted on beat 4 ("Now the").

5 This measure's time signature is 3/4, and the vocals begin on beat 1. Then, to p.87, 4th system, m.1.

6 After this measure, to p.87, 4th system, m.3.

GET BACK

Words and Music by JOHN LENNON
and PAUL McCARTNEY

The version of the song released on "Anthology 3" differs from the standard version, printed here, as annotated.

1 In the "Anthology 3" version, after the Verse 3 instrumental solo, to p.88, 2nd system, m.2 for Verse 4 ("Sweet Loretta Martin").

Get back!_ Get back_ to where you once be-longed._ Get back!_

Get back!_ Get back_ to where you once be-longed._

[2] After the Verse 2 instrumental solo, to the 4th ending. After p.89, 3rd system, m.3, the "Anthology 3" version returns to p.88, 2nd system, m.2 for the Verse 3 instrumental solo.

1,2,3 A | 4 no chord

(Get back, Jo Jo)

Spoken ad lib:

Get back, Loretta, your momma's waitin' for you
Wearin' her high heel shoes and a low neck sweater.
Get back home, Loretta.

Repeat and Fade

[3] After Verse 4, to the 1st ending. Then, the "Anthology 3" version returns to p.88, 2nd system, m.2 for the Verse 5 instrumental solo.

[4] After Verse 5, to the 4th ending. After p.89, 3rd system, m.3, the "Anthology 3" version goes to p.89, 4th system, m.1.

[5] These four measures are repeated once, then to p.89, 1st system, m.1. The "Anthology 3" version then continues, takes the fourth ending, and ends with p.89, 3rd system, m.2.

SOMETHING
(SUPPLEMENT)

Slowly

You know I love ___ that wom-an of mine, ___ and I need ___ her ___ all of the time. ___ No, I'm tell-ing you ___ that wom - an, that wom-an don't make ___ me blue. ___

To p.91, 1st system, m.2

1 This is a transcription of an additional verse in the "Anthology 3" version. The original key is A major. This section replaces the first 3 systems of p.93. The "Anthology 3" version then returns to p.91, 1st system, m.2 for Verse 3 ("Something in the way she knows").

SOMETHING

Words and Music by
GEORGE HARRISON

The version of the song released on "Anthology 3" differs from the standard version, printed here, as annotated.

1 The "Anthology 3" version is in A major.

2 The "Anthology 3" version begins with 2 measures of A major and then continues with this measure.

3 "Anthology 3" Verse 2 lyrics: "Something in her smile."

4 After Verse 3, to the 1st ending, then to p.91, 1st system, m.2. The vocals are omitted until p.91, 3rd system, m.3, beat 4 ("You know I believe").

5 After Verse 4, to p.93, 4th system, m.3.

6 The first three systems on this page have been replaced with an additional verse in the "Anthology 3" version. See supplement for a transcription of this verse.

COME AND GET IT

Words and Music by
PAUL McCARTNEY

The version of the song released on "Anthology 3" differs from the standard version, printed here, as annotated.

1 The "Anthology 3" version is in E major.

Will you walk a - way from a fool and his mo — ney —— If you
want it, here — it is, Come and get it but you bet-ter hur -ry 'cos it's go-ing fast —
If you
Son - ny if you want it here — it is, Come and get it, but you bet-ter
(tacet--------------)

To Coda

D.%. al Coda

CODA

2 The chord on beat 1 is E major.

BECAUSE

Words and Music by JOHN LENNON
and PAUL McCARTNEY

Ah.

Be -
cause
cause the world is round, it turns me
the wind is high, it blows my
cause the sky is blue, it makes me

The version of the song released on "Anthology 3" differs from the standard version, printed here, as annotated.

1 The "Anthology 3" mix begins in this measure and only presents the vocal tracks.

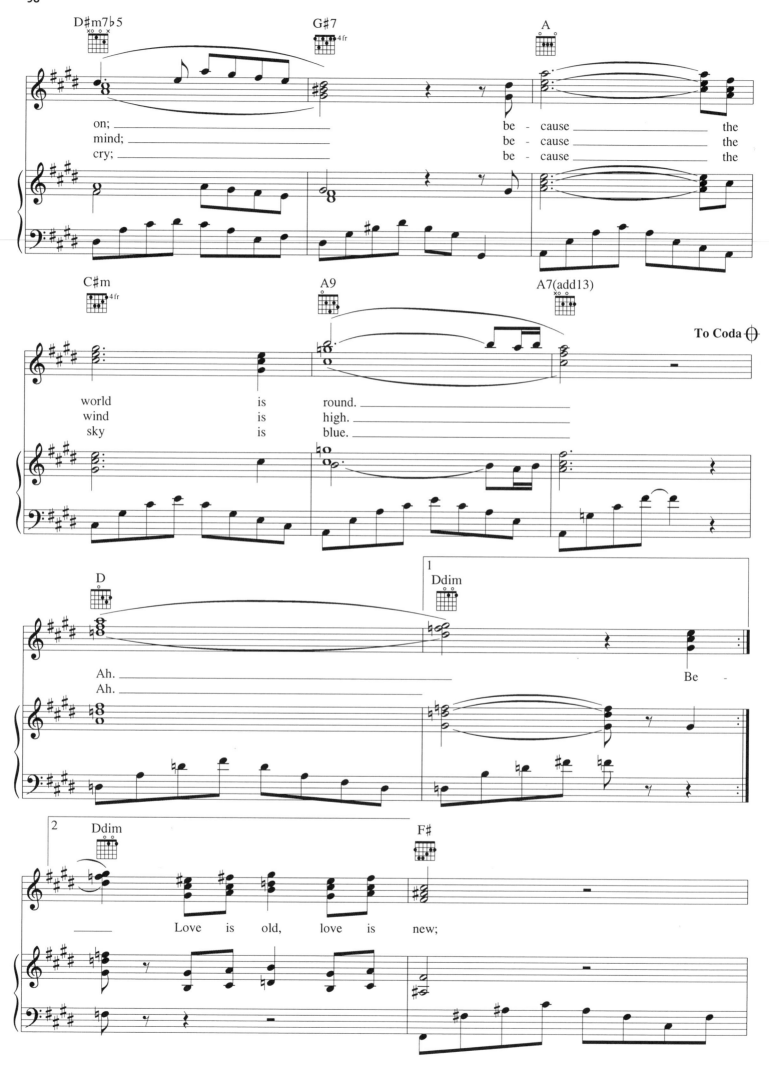

LET IT BE

Words and Music by JOHN LENNON
and PAUL McCARTNEY

[1] The "Anthology 3" version begins with p.103, 4th system, m.2 and p.104, 1st system, m.1. The vocals from p.100, 2nd system, m.1 ("When I") are sung in p.104, 1st system, m.1. The song then continues at p.100, 2nd system, m.2 ("Find myself in times of trouble").

When I find my-self___ in times of trou-ble

Instrumental

Moth-er Mar-y comes to me Speak-ing words of wis-dom, Let it be___ and in my hour of dark-ness She is

The version of the song released on "Anthology 3" differs from the standard version, printed here, as annotated.

3 "Anthology 3" Verse 2 lyrics: "And in my hour of darkness, she is standing right in front of me."

4 "Anthology 3" Verse 1 lyrics: "Still a chance for them to see."

[5] "Anthology 3" lyrics: "Whisper words of wisdom."

[6] The order of the verses is reversed in the "Anthology 3" version.

7 After this measure, to p.104, 4th system, m.2. "Let it be" is spoken on beat 4 of that measure.

THE END
(SUPPLEMENT)

[1] This is a transcription of the beginning of the "Anthology 3" version. This version then continues with p.108, 3rd system, m.1 ("Love you, love you").

THE END

Words and Music by JOHN LENNON
and PAUL McCARTNEY

The version of the song released on "Anthology 3" differs from the standard version, printed here, as annotated.

1 See supplement for the beginning of the "Anthology 3" version.

Love you, ___ love you, ___

love you, ____ love you, ____

love you, ____ love you, ____

love you, ____ love you, ____

love you, ____ love you, ____